Homeless Students

by Cynthia Crosson Tower
Donna J. White

nea PROFESSIONAL LIBRARY
National Education Association
Washington, D.C.

Authors' Acknowledgments

The work and dedication of numerous people have made this monograph possible. Our thanks to Claire Angers, Cynthia LeBlanc, Joan Freedman, and Richard LaBelle, who shared their experiences as educators deeply concerned about homeless children. We also recognize Michelle Fryt and Edward Smith for the information they provided. And we appreciate the enthusiasm of the students of the "Working with the Homeless" class at Fitchburg State College for bringing the authors together and for giving us the idea for the project. To Major Victor Tidman and the staff of the Salvation Army Booth Home for their support and concern, we are grateful. We thank our typist, Muriel Crosson, who gave us numerous hours of her time. Finally, we thank the homeless parents and children who agreed to talk with us and to share their lives so that others could learn about their plight. It is to these families and to all homeless children that we dedicate our efforts in the hope that this publication will make a small contribution to bettering their lives.

Printing History
First Printing: September 1989

Note

The opinions expressed in this publication should not be construed as representing the policy or position of the National Education Association. Materials published by the NEA Professional Library are intended to be discussion documents for educators who are concerned with specialized interests of the profession.

Library of Congress Cataloging-in Publication Data

Tower, Cynthia Crosson.
    Homeless students.

    Bibliography: p.
    1. Homeless students—United States. 2. Homeless students—Education—United States. I. White, Donna J.
II. Title
LC5144.2.T68   1989   371.96'7   89–12481
    ISBN 0–8106–0245–8

CONTENTS

The Authors

Cynthia Crosson Tower is Professor in the Human Services Program, Behavioral Science Department, Fitchburg State College, Massachusetts. Dr. Tower is the author of *How Schools Can Help Combat Child Abuse and Neglect,* published by NEA, and the developer of *Child Abuse and Neglect: The NEA In-Service Training Program.*

Donna J. White is Director of the Salvation Army Booth Home, a shelter serving homeless families in Leominster, Massachusetts.

The Advisory Panel

Susan M. Chaffin, Retired Guidance Counselor, Ithaca High School, Michigan

Audry McKenna Lynch, Guidance Counselor, Bernal Intermediate School, San Jose, California

Richard D. Scheffler, Language Arts Teacher, Northbrook Middle School, Mendota, Illinois

Denis P. Sicchitano, School Counselor, Boiling Springs Junior-Senior High School, Pennsylvania

Charles W. Smith, Associate Professor, Department of Educational Psychology, Counseling and Special Education, Northern Illinois University, DeKalb

INTRODUCTION

Why do teachers need to know about homelessness?

> Nine-year-old Leah listened intently to the voice of the volunteer who came to the homeless shelter weekly to read to and entertain the children.
> "I have a favorite story," piped up Leah when the current book was completed.
> "Which one," queried the young volunteer.
> "*The Wizard of Oz*," Leah answered.
> "And what is your favorite part?"
> Leah's eyes grew tearful as she replied in an almost inaudible voice:
> "My favorite part is at the end when Dorothy says, 'There's no place like home.' "

Most people often take their home for granted, but for Leah who had been shuffled from shelter to shelter, a home is a dream she cherishes and hopes someday to realize.

But a home is not all that homeless students need. There is more to their problem than four walls and a roof they can call their own. By the time they find their dream of stability—if in fact they ever do—homeless students have been stigmatized, humiliated, and often denied the quality of education we in the United States consider to be our human right. Teachers can, however, help children like Leah experience the joy of learning.

There are several reasons why teachers should become more aware of issues surrounding the problem of homelessness: (1) large numbers of students are now homeless; (2) teachers need to respond quickly to the educational needs of their students; (3) teachers who understand students' problems may be able to provide one thing homeless students need most—a safe and secure environment; (4) teachers may need to educate others in order to help provide space for the homeless student to learn; and (5) educators have been and can continue to be forerunners of social change.

---

*Numbers in parentheses appearing in the text refer to the Bibliography beginning on page 46.

5

THE NUMBERS

Today homeless families are the fastest-growing population in the United States. Of the estimated three to four million homeless people, over 40 percent are families. A large percentage (estimated to be 40 percent) of the children of these families do not attend school (13). Their reasons vary. An itinerant lifestyle makes regular attendance difficult. Children who do attend tend to feel "different"; they are often teased or ridiculed by their peers.

> Mike demonstrated the feelings of many homeless students when he refused to have his picture taken by a local newspaper. The reporter hoped that his story would publicize the efforts of the area's homeless shelter. "This might be a nice place," Mike told a volunteer after the reporter had left, "but who wants the whole world to know you don't have no place to live but here?"

Jonathan Kozol outlines the plight of homeless children through interviews with families who live in welfare hotels (12). Of the total homeless population Kozol estimates that in New York City alone, there are 18,000 homeless parents and children in 5,000 families (p. 4). The District of Columbia's Pitts Hotel, housing over 500 families nightly, has also been highly publicized (and criticized) for its deplorable conditions and inadequate facilities (12, p. 90).

It is easy for the statistics to become faceless numbers—for homeless problems to be seen as some phenomena happening "out there," but not touching our own lives. Yet, increasingly, teachers report finding more and more students who describe the horrors of homelessness.

"When five of the 25 children in my class gave the same address, I began to wonder," reported one teacher. "I soon discovered that 380 Beach Street was the address of the homeless shelter." The sheer numbers of homeless students make it mandatory that teachers prepare to teach them.

RESPONDING QUICKLY

Not only must teachers be armed with knowledge about the homeless to meet the needs of increasing numbers of homeless students, but they are being forced to respond quickly and creatively to the issues that homelessness creates. The itinerant nature of homeless families and the short stays allowed by shelters (usually between 30 and 90 days) mean that students move from school to school. Consequently, there is often little or no time to undertake lengthy educational evaluation. "By the time we got the referral for education assessment in motion," commented an elementary school principal, "the child had left the school."

Thus teachers and the schools in which they teach must be able to do quick, informal assessments of students' needs until more formal means are possible. Such informal responses require basic knowledge about homeless students and their families, what they experience, and why they find themselves in this situation.

PROVIDING A SAFE AND SECURE ENVIRONMENT

As teachers begin to recognize the pressures placed upon homeless families, they realize that the children are denied security and stability. For Leah "a home" meant that she would feel safe and secure. Since homeless parents who have histories of abuse and instability are caught up in the logistics of survival, it is often difficult for them to provide a safe atmosphere for their children. The school may be the only haven in the child's life—however brief the attendance. Teachers who understand what homeless children have experienced and know how to respond to them are better able to provide the warmth and nurturing these students so desperately need.

TEACHING OTHERS

Part of the homeless experience for these students involves being stigmatized and often taunted by other children. The informed teacher will be able to sensitize others to the issue of homelessness and, it is hoped, minimize some of the pressure homeless students feel from their peers.

Nor are peers the only ones who may need to be sensitized to the issues facing homeless students. Colleagues, administrators, and community leaders often benefit from additional knowledge shared with them by an informed teacher.

CONTRIBUTING TO SOCIAL CHANGE AND SOLUTIONS

As with so many other issues (e.g., child abuse, drug abuse), teachers are in an ideal position to gain, through classroom experience, a better picture of the needs of homeless students and to be instrumental in meeting those needs. As they learn how to address these students' unique problems, teachers can more easily suggest, design, or institute new programs that will make education as available to these learners as it is to others.

7

Since understanding homeless students and their families is the beginning of the teacher's response to the problem, this monograph is designed to acquaint the teacher with the variety of issues involved in being homeless. Chapter 1 provides a brief history of homelessness and an explanation of why so many families today are undergoing this trauma. Chapter 2 gives a picture of homeless students and their families. Chapter 3 describes some of the problems these students may have in the classroom and suggests ways to address these problems. Chapter 4 discusses what teachers can do to help beyond the classroom setting. The emphasis throughout these pages is the importance of educators taking a proactive stance on a problem that promises to get worse before it gets better. The monograph, then, sets the groundwork for helping the homeless student both now and in the future.

Chapter 1

WHY ARE STUDENTS HOMELESS?
A BRIEF LOOK AT THE PROBLEM

There have always been people who were homeless. The problem may have been called by a different name or may have been dealt with in different ways, but the fact is that homelessness has existed through the centuries. Many people remember the vagrants or tramps of several decades ago—men who sometimes begged or asked for odd jobs to earn a few dollars to buy food. Vagrants—people who often had problems such as alcoholism or some form of mental or physical disorder—were treated with varying degrees of indulgence. During the mid-1800s, most of these homeless had the option of being taken in by families who might receive a small fee from the town for their care. Later, they were kept overnight in police stations, which became the first kind of shelter (4). Tramps, on the other hand, were a mobile force of workers who mined, lumbered, herded, harvested, or performed any number of jobs, traveling from place to place wherever they could find work.

In the late 1890s society began to react to the phenomenon of the homeless in a more organized manner than sheltering them in police stations, families, or churches. By 1894, New York City had 105 lodging houses to accommodate 16,000 homeless for a fee as small as three to thirty-five cents a night. But shelters like these were far from adequate or even sanitary; therefore other solutions were sought (4)

Then, an increased demand for unskilled workers by new factories and agricultural enterprises seemed to lessen the problem somewhat. The next period that stands out in history was the 1930s when economic depression forced many to join the ranks of the unemployed and sometimes inevitable homelessness. At this time, the complexion of homelessness began to change.

Certainly there were homeless families before the great depression, but society seemed to have found ways to provide for mothers and children. Some were boarded with other families, some were relegated to poorhouses. But arrangements always seemed possible to make when children were involved.

The 1930s presented a different problem by virtue of the sheer numbers of the poor. Emergency shelters were made available for families as well as for transient men. Between 1929 and 1932 the number of families using emergency shelters increased from 6,902 to 55,789 (24). Then the New Deal programs mobilized resources and welfare reforms that began to provide funds or services for these families. Over the years, poor families became eligible for public assistance payments, housing assistance, and even rent subsidies.

In the 1980s homelessness once again emerged as a real problem not only for the unemployed, the mentally ill, and the returned veteran, but also for entire families. Cutbacks in federal welfare programs in the early years of the decade reduced funds to support Aid to Families with Dependent Children (AFDC), food stamps, and nutrition programs, so that more families were forced to stretch their dollars, sometimes having to make choices between buying food and paying rent (10). Many contend that one of the major reasons for today's homeless problem is the lack of affordable housing. Kozol (12) cites the fact that in New York City alone, rents have risen to the point where many families must pay over three-quarters of their income for housing. Older, affordable housing is being torn down or converted to businesses or condominiums. In areas that once housed low-income families, property is being bought up by young professionals who renovate the buildings and sell or rent them for prices far beyond the means of the former residents. The average job available for the unskilled worker who heads a family nets about $450 a month. While such a salary might pay the rent in the few low-income neighborhoods that remain, little will be left for food and clothing, let alone allowances for illness or catastrophes (12).

Until recently, departments of children's services considered lack of housing a reason to place children in foster care. Finally, society realizes the importance of allowing children to remain with their families, even if the family becomes homeless. Homeless children do not need the additional trauma of separation from their families. But those who remain with their families create new problems, many of which are discussed in the following pages.

Most discussions of the homeless mention shelters, welfare hotels, living on the street, and living with friends (see Glossary). What actually constitutes a homeless family? The Office of Program Evaluation and Research of the Ohio Department of Mental Health has developed a particularly inclusive definition.

Homeless families or youths are those who—

1. Have limited or no shelter for any length of time (e.g., sleeping in

10

cars, abandoned buildings, on the street.

2. Live in shelters or missions run by religious or state organizations for any length of time (e.g., shelters run by the Salvation Army, Volunteers of America).

3. Live in cheap hotels/motels, when the length of stay is 45 days or less.

4. Live in other unique facilities for 45 days or less (e.g., tents, with friends, at campgrounds, in shacks. (19, p. 5)

Whether we define the circumstances of homelessness or cite statistics, the homeless have faces. The children of the homeless have needs—physical, social, emotional, spiritual, and educational. These needs will be considered in the following chapters.

Chapter 2

A PICTURE OF HOMELESS STUDENTS AND THEIR FAMILIES

ITINERANT FAMILIES

Seven-year-old Doria spoke easily of her itinerant years:

"Daddy used to pick stuff—any fruit or vegetables what needed pickin'. Then he left and Ma and Juan [her three-year-old brother] and me took our car and came up north. Ma said she had relatives up here, but we couldn't find them. We stayed in the car until it wouldn't go no more. We didn't have no money, see?"

In fact, Doria's family had traveled north with another family of four—all camping out by the roadside at night. When they reached the frigid temperatures of March in New England, they took up lodging for a short time with friends of the other family. But this arrangement was short-lived. The three-room apartment was too crowded and tensions grew until Doria's 22-year-old mother took her two children and left with her only major possession, a run-down car. For several nights the family lived in the vehicle, parking in alleys and behind buildings. Sometimes the police would force them to move on. On the fifth night, an officer noticed the shivering children and after questioning the mother took the family to a local homeless shelter. For the last two months, Doria, her mother, and her brother have been staying there while the shelter staff seeks out resources to help the struggling family.

Being itinerant is not new for children of homeless families—nor is constant crisis. While lack of affordable housing and few suitable paying jobs are thought to be largely responsible for the current homeless problem, studies show that for most of these families, homelessness is the latest in a long string of crises. (See Figure 1.) A recent study undertaken at the Urban Family Center (UFC) in New York City found that in addition to financial need and inadequate housing, most families experienced problems in the functioning of various family members. Ninety-six percent of the mothers in this study were having difficulty maintaining their roles adequately. The families were also besieged by

12

many types of stress such as serious illness of a family member (30 percent of families), death of a close family member (25 percent), pregnancy (33 percent), or separation from a husband or boyfriend (31 percent). One-third of the mothers described mental illness or "problems with their nerves," while 19 percent had a history of psychiatric hospitalization. Forty-three percent of the mothers interviewed had never been married (15, pp. 49–50).

The Child Welfare League of America (CWLA) studied 163 homeless families with 340 children. Most parents were employed but felt the stresses of being unable to find or pay for housing. For this reason many parents were forced to turn to governmental programs such as Aid to Families with Dependent Children (AFDC) or housing authorities (for subsidized housing) to postpone homelessness (13). For those who became homeless, the supports seemed to be exhausted.

Perhaps unprepared for parenthood, the mothers in these homeless families feel pressured. Many of the mothers are young (the mean age is 29 years in the UFC study) when the average family is relatively large (the mean number of children is three). Many mothers (65 percent) had their first child before they were 20-years-old. Homelessness also drives families apart. It was not uncommon for mothers to be forced to leave young children elsewhere—between 22 and 50 percent of the families in the CWLA and UFC studies, respectively, had children living elsewhere (13).

MIGRANT FAMILIES

One unique population that might technically be considered homeless consists of the children of migrant workers. Although their itinerant lifestyle is a direct response to nature's timeclock that regulates the harvesting of a variety of fruits and vegetables, migrant children often suffer the same education deprivation and social problems as the homeless children. According to the Migrant Student Transfer System (MSTS) records in Little Rock, Arkansas, there are approximately 530,856 migrant students accounted for across the nation. Increasingly, they are coming from Spanish-speaking families (11). (See Figure 2.) The language barrier often compounds attempts to provide these students with the education they deserve.

Migrant children face many of the same problems experienced by other homeless children. Their families—largely uneducated—may even attempt to leave the migrant work force. Typically, their marginal skills and limited education make it difficult for them to find more stable employment. Their only recourse seems to be to return to field work.

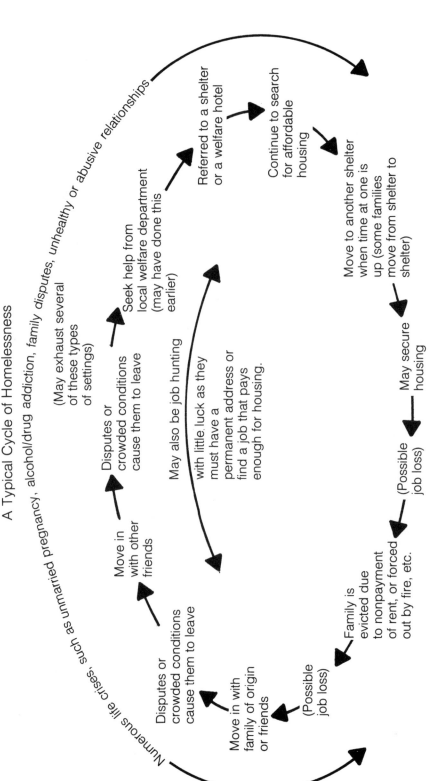

Figure 1
A Typical Cycle of Homelessness

Numerous life crisis, such as unmarried pregnancy, alcohol/drug addiction, family disputes, unhealthy or abusive relationships

(May exhaust several of these types of settings)

Seek help from local welfare department (may have done this earlier)

Referred to a shelter or a welfare hotel

Continue to search for affordable housing

Move to another shelter when time at one is up (some families move from shelter to shelter)

Disputes or crowded conditions cause them to leave

Move in with other friends

May also be job hunting

with little luck as they must have a permanent address or find a job that pays enough for housing.

May secure housing

Disputes or crowded conditions cause them to leave

Move in with family of origin or friends

(Possible job loss)

(Possible job loss)

Family is evicted due to nonpayment of rent, or forced out by fire, etc.

The picture of homelessness is complex

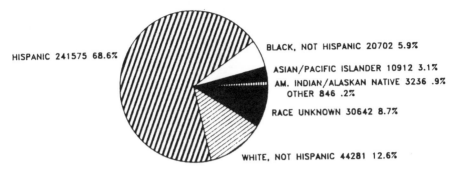

Figure 2
Distribution of Migrant Students
by Racial/Ethnic Membership

HISPANIC 241575 68.6%

BLACK, NOT HISPANIC 20702 5.9%

ASIAN/PACIFIC ISLANDER 10912 3.1%
AM. INDIAN/ALASKAN NATIVE 3236 .9%
OTHER 846 .2%

RACE UNKNOWN 30642 8.7%

WHITE, NOT HISPANIC 44281 12.6%

SOURCE: *Migrant Education: A Consolidated View* (Denver, Colo.: Interstate Migrant Education Council, n. d.). From U. S. Department of Education, Migrant Performance Reports 1984–1985.

In his classic study of migrant children, Coles (5) comments:

> I fear that . . . migrant children do indeed become what some of their harshest and least forgiving critics call them: listless, apathetic, hard to understand, disorderly, subject to outbursts of self-injury and destructive violence toward others, and on and on. I fear it is no small thing, a disaster almost beyond repair, when children grow up, literally, adrift, on the land, when they learn as a birthright the disorder and early sorrow that goes with virtual peonage, with an unsettled, vagabond life. (p. 76)

Migrant children experience the poor nutrition, the growing up too fast, the instability, and the unpredictability that other homeless children experience, but because their condition is more an accepted way of life for their parents, there are differences. Preschool migrant children are actually able to be closer to their parents. They often roam freely in the fields as they grow up. They do not face the same hazards as inner-city children. They watch their parents engaged in hurried work and translate their observations into an impulsive, impatient lifestyle. Coles (5) maintains that, by school age, these children begin to feel drained by the hectic pace. In addition, as they have learned to move from field to field, they move from task to task often leaving the first unfinished—and with little sense of accomplishment. The difficulty they have keeping up with peers seemingly attests to the fact that they cannot keep pace. Studies show that children of migrant workers are from six to eigh-

15

teen months behind expected grade levels for their age groups (11).

The poorly educated parents may value education little and can be of little help in their children's studying. Certainly these students perceive that in a society that values success and education, their parents are probably not highly regarded. Thus the children often feel forced to choose between education—which if not geared to their needs may make them feel like failures—or the only lifestyle and security they have known—their parents'.

ETHNIC/RACIAL FACTORS

Ethnically and racially, the picture of the homeless varies (see Table 1). The UFC study found that most of the families were Black (67 percent) or Hispanic (24 percent), while the CWLA researchers reported that 46 percent of the families were white, 32 percent Black, 17 percent Hispanic, 2 percent American Indian, and 3 percent of unknown racial and ethnic background (15, 13). Certainly the geographic area of the study would affect these figures. The Boston study (2) found that 48 percent of the families were white, 45 percent Black, and only 6 percent Hispanic.

Table 1
Ethnic/Racial Origin of Homeless Families

	NYC (UFC study) (175 families)	CWLA* (163 families)	Boston (82 families, 156 children)
White	9%(not specified)	46%	48%
Black	67%	32%	45%
Hispanic	24%	17%	6%
American Indian	—	2%	—
Other		3%	1%

*Covered eight cities: Washington, D.C.; Tampa, Florida; Detroit, Michigan; Salt Lake City, Utah; San Francisco, California; Los Angeles, California, Houston; Texas.

SOURCES: Adapted from Phillips, M., and others, "Homeless Families: Services Make a Difference" (*Social Casework,* January 1981, pp. 48–53); Maza P. L., and Hall, J. A., *Homeless Children and Their Families: A Preliminary Study* (Child Welfare League of America, 1988); and Bassuk, E., Rubin, L., and Lauriat, A. S., "Characteristics of Sheltered Homeless Families" (*American Journal of Public Health,* September 1986, pp. 1097–1101).

EFFECTS OF HOMELESSNESS ON CHILDREN

The demographics present a global picture of homeless children, but what of the children themselves? Often these young people have been born into crisis-ridden families. As homeless advocate, Steve Miller, states, "Homelessness isn't an event. It is a process."

Herbie's mother, Olga, had been hospitalized for her manic depressive (bipolar) illness three times before Herbie was five. The child of alcoholic parents, Olga drifted from job to job and boyfriend to boyfriend between hospitalizations. When she was hospitalized, her sister cared for Herbie. The sister had six children of her own and a husband who came in and out of the household frequently so that no one knew when he would be there. Herbie enjoyed his aunt's home, however. His aunt's behavior was relatively predictable. Although he loved his mother, he wasn't always sure what to expect from her. It was his aunt who took him to school the first day and his aunt who came to the parent-teacher conference. But things were far from ideal. When Herbie's uncle returned, he was usually physically abusive to his wife and on occasion to his children as well.

Soon after Herbie's sixth birthday his mother, newly released from the hospital, came to live with the family in the five-room apartment. She shared Herbie's bed and told him excitedly how they would find a place of their own. Day after day she searched for an apartment and a job. The job became a reality when she began to waitress at a local fast-food chain, but the apartment never materialized. Instead, Olga would come home with magazines depicting beautiful houses and apartments and dream with the boy of the home they would have. After six weeks Herbie's aunt said she could no longer stand her sister's "spacey behavior." She gave her a week to find an apartment. At the end of a week Olga, in a fit of anger, left her sister's home with her small son. One night at her parent's home proved no better. Mother and son left at three in the morning amidst a drunken fight between her parents. Frightened, Herbie clung to his mother while the pair slept in an alley—a location that would be their "bed" for several weeks, until Olga's deteriorating behavior brought them to the attention of the police and eventually to a homeless shelter.

For Herbie, life was punctuated by alcoholism, domestic violence, instability, and mental illness. He was frightened, confused, and unsure of where to call home. Was home with his aunt's noisy brood, with the various boyfriends with whom his mother had lived, or by the side of his equally confused and ill mother?

Emotional / Psychological Reactions

Such feelings of *confusion* in a child are typical. Homeless children *feel hopeless and out of control of their lives*. They need to check in, periodically, to make sure that their parents are still there. Some call the shelter regularly. Others, like John, exhibit behavior that necessitates their parents' coming to the school for them.

John, 10, is the victim of a broken home. His mother, an alcoholic, has traveled with him from place to place for the last several years. John's father has kept periodic contact. Eventually John and his mother took up temporary residence in a homeless shelter. His father soon found them and requested that he take John from time to time. On one such occasion the father, who had some difficulty with responsibility himself, was told by the mother and the shelter staff to return John no later than five o'clock. When five arrived and John had not returned, his mother became distraught. Deciding to search for father and son, she combed every spot she could think of. Then, overwhelmed by her worry, she stopped at a local bar for a drink. Upon finally returning to the shelter, she found her son. Sobbing uncontrollably she told him that he had caused her to drink and now face the possibility of being asked to leave the shelter for violating the rules.

The next day the school called the shelter saying that the mother should pick up John who had been vomiting most of the day. Mother was greeted by her near-hysterical son who sobbed, "Ma, I'm so glad you're O.K., I was so worried."

Physical and Behavioral Manifestations

It is not uncommon for children like John to exhibit *physical manifestations* of *their confusion and worry*. John's vomiting appeared to be indicative of his concerns about home rather than an actual illness. Stress *can* give rise to illness. The CWLA study found that as a result of "the brief interview, without the assistance of medical personnel, agency workers were able to detect an immediate need for health care in ten percent of the children" (3). Need for health care comes not only from the child's being under severe stress, but also because medical attention is frequently not given for small complaints that can escalate. Sores, cuts, rashes, hypothermia, and lice may go untreated as parents lack the financial resources, are afraid to seek help, or are distracted by weightier concerns.

It is also true that homeless children often feel a need to "take care" of their parent(s). Children are perceptive; they are also experts in observation. It becomes clear to them very early that parents are not equipped

18

to handle the situation they find themselves in. The immature, needy parent therefore often turns to relatively young children for support. Out of necessity these children *learn survival skills* and *perceive that they "need" to care for their parents*, emotionally or even physically, in many circumstances.

> Jane Hart was suffering from acute hypothermia and pneumonia when she was brought to the emergency room of the local hospital by a neighborhood worker and the police. The police were called more to restrain 11-year-old Darren than to help medics with his mother. Residents of a dumpster, mother and son had been homeless for several months. When Jane became ill, Darren had cared for her, bringing food he found in trash cans. When the weather became cold, she scavenged for rags and newspapers to cover them. Finally Darren stole a blanket. The store owner who observed the theft notified a local service center. "I thought that a kid who would steal a blanket must really need it. Most kids would steal something they could sell," the storekeeper told the outreach worker. From the merchant's description, the worker found Darren and his ailing mother. So fiercely protective was the boy of his parent that police were summoned to help.

By virtue of the lives they lead, both homeless teenagers and children in homeless families often demonstrate *poor hygiene*. Once in a shelter they find that most facilities require guests to bathe and maintain adequate cleanliness. But habits developed during years of neglect and a multitude of pressures are difficult to break.

Malnutrition is another curse of the homeless child. On their own, families and youths with some money purchase the most available and least expensive fare—food usually lacking in essential nutrients. Shelters try to provide balanced meals, but deprivation and a chaotic lifestyle may have colored tastes and preferences of both children and adults.

As a result not only of their lifestyle but also of dietary limitations, children and youths can be *listless and withdrawn*. *Depression* is a common companion. Bassuk and Rubin (1) found depression to be one of the most pervasive factors in their study of 156 children in Massachusetts family shelters. Depressed children may be fatigued—symptomatic of insufficient sleep and inconsistent routines as well as anxiousness over their future. Children in families also mirror their parents' anxiety.

For some children, depression and stress get translated into *hyperactivity*, an inability to stay within the structure of rules, and often *aggressive, hostile behavior*.

> A teacher who found eight-year-old Roy vandalizing the school corridor with a can of spray paint and a knife enlisted the help of the

school counselor to talk with him. "I hate it here," Roy blurted out. "If I trash it, I can move."

The story eventually emerged that Roy's family had lived in numerous housing projects. Roy's older brother, an extremely disturbed adolescent, had done much damage to their various residences. Because the rent was paid by welfare, the family was never charged for damages but was evicted on numerous occasions. Roy's mother, overwhelmed by her oldest son's behavior, felt powerless to stop it. Now the family moved from apartment to apartment. Currently they resided in a shelter, having exhausted the good graces of local landlords. Thus Roy had learned the usefulness of vandalism and found such acts an outlet for his own anger.

Homeless children are subject not only to violent dysfunctional homes but are also vulnerable to abuses from outsiders. Kozol (12) describes a conversation with a young girl living in a welfare hotel in New York City:

One day we were out in Herald Square. This old man, a white man, he say he was goin' to give me money. Gave me a five dollar bill. Then he ask me was I hungry and I was, so he says he is goin' to take me to Burger King. So I went with him and we went to this parking lot and he pulled down his drawers. I came home. (p. 77)

Children on the street are vulnerable to sexual abuse or to pimps searching for new "employees."

Many homeless children *daydream* of better times to come. Younger children and teens fantasize, and sometimes in their desperate need for normalcy, these fantasies seem to feel like reality.

Clara told apparently preposterous stories of her family's affluent past. Reminiscent of old Shirley Temple movies, Clara described herself as the "poor little rich girl, fallen on hard times." Her teachers found her fantasies unnerving and saw her as a disturbed and pathological liar. Counseling uncovered that she was well aware of the differences between her life and her fantasies but was desperately clinging to her childlike dreams in hopes of better times.

ADOLESCENTS

While younger children are homeless along with their families, many older children are completely on their own. Adolescent victims of dysfunctional families, alcoholism, drug abuse, and child abuse and neglect are especially vulnerable to homelessness.

"My parents threw me out when I was 13," recounts Noreen. "I stole some money from my mother's purse before I left and took a bus to another city. I wanted as far away from them as possible." Noreen became a prostitute, convincing some of her clients to let her stay with them. Eventually she was picked up by a pimp who set her up in business. At 16 she was a seasoned prostitute.

Virgil, on the other hand, ran away when he was 15. A victim of sexual and physical abuse by his father, Virgil decided that his only recourse was to leave. Very early he made friends with several street people who advised him how to live on the streets. Bouncing from various shelters to friends' houses to sleeping on the street, Virgil managed to maintain his lifestyle for over a year. A boy who looked older than his age, he would occasionally volunteer for a work-a-day program. Through occasional day jobs he managed to survive until he was approached sexually by a man in a public restroom. Overcome with flashbacks of his father's abuse, Virgil beat the man severely and left him. A day later he was arrested.

Homeless teenagers are more often noticed for their deviant behavior than for their homelessness. A report on homeless youth by the Ninety-sixth Congress estimated that programs serviced up to 10,000 homeless youths a year while the total population of such teenagers was estimated to be between 100,000 and 400,000 (6). According to estimates, this number has grown significantly. Drugs, too, claim teenagers for the streets.

Robert, age 15, is a victim of parents who are addicted to both drugs and alcohol. His father was always the one to whom Robert looked for support. When his dad was indicted for a crime and sent to jail, Robert's world crumbled around him. An excellent student, he quit school in despair and was befriended by a group of young people who lived on their own, selling drugs. Now hooked on both drugs and alcohol, Robert roams from shelter to detoxification center to detention center only to be released to complete the cycle again.

Price (17) contends that street youths have unique ways of maintaining themselves on the street—often independent of shelters:

Frequently they band together and sleep in adandoned buildings downtown. They tend to be secretive even among themselves about the location of the "empties" as they call them. As more youths find out about a new empty they must be included, since anyone denied admission might disclose the building to the authorities. Thus, to discover another's empty is tantamount to gaining entry to the group. (17, p. 24)

As the group increases in size, members tend to look for new space, often expanding to areas of the building that are condemned and therefore unsafe and more likely to result in physical injuries. Fire also becomes a hazard as youths in deserted buildings use matches or candles to light the darkness. Since alcohol and drugs are often part of their lifestyles, poor judgment and impaired coordination may result in starting fires (17).

Itinerant youths may also live in cars, all-night movie houses, hospital emergency waiting rooms, churches, subway stations, or in parks. Some find unique ways to clothe and feed themselves.

> Larry attended high school regularly. His clothes began to puzzle his homeroom teacher, however. Although they appeared clean, they were often too small or too large, and were always a different outfit. The teacher eventually learned from another student that Larry lived on the street. The clothes he wore were stolen from laundromats where he would abandon his old clothes. He ate either at shelters and soup kitchens or by stealing bits of food from markets. Unlike many of his counterparts, however, Larry stayed free of drugs, allowing himself an occasional smoke of marijuana or a beer when these could be obtained. He loved school and was determined to finish despite the lifestyle that he worked to keep secret.

Unlike Larry, many street youths drop out of school. Those who do remain, however, become masters of deceit in an attempt to cover their lifestyles.

Whether migrant or inner-city homeless, younger child or adolescent, the needs of these students can sometimes seem overwhelming to school personnel. These needs often translate into behavior and impediments that challenge the classroom teacher. Chapter 3 discusses these problems and suggests ways for teachers to respond to them.

Chapter 3

PROBLEMS OF HOMELESS STUDENTS IN THE CLASSROOM: HOW THE TEACHER CAN RESPOND

The homeless student's problems in school can be grouped into four overlapping and interrelated areas:

- Problems in transition
- Problems with studies
- Problems with peers
- Problems with self-concept.

This chapter discusses each of these problems in turn. It also provides examples and suggestions to help teachers as they work with the homeless students in their classrooms.

Two tables summarize many aspects of these problems. Table 2 gives three types of symptoms that homeless students exhibit—those that are visible from students' appearance, those that are discernible from their behavior, and those that are manifested in problems in school. Table 3 lists typical frustrations experienced by homeless students and their teachers and other school personnel.

PROBLEMS IN TRANSITION

Nothing can be more frustrating for the school system, and especially for the teacher, than to find in midterm a new student about whom nothing is known. There are no records from a previous school, no letters from those who know of the student's abilities, and often no parents with time or energy to supply any details. (See Appendix C for a sample Student Assessment Form, which can be very helpful in such cases.) The student may be withdrawn and quiet, offering little information.

One of the biggest problems faced by schools is that the system of school transfer often does not work for homeless children. The student may have left the previous school quickly or unexpectedly, with little or no opportunity to set the transfer process into motion. The parent may not have realized the necessity of transferring records, or did not know

Table 2
Symptoms of Homeless Students

Visible Symptoms	Behavior	Problems in School
• Malnutrition • Poor hygiene • Unattended medical needs • Unattended dental needs • Poor health, especially skin rashes, respiratory problems, asthma • Neglect • Abuse • Involvement with drugs	• Low self-esteem • Withdrawn or listless or • Hostile and aggressive • Tired • Emotionally needy • Difficulty in trusting • Hoards food • Parentified (takes care of parents) • Old beyond their years • Fantasize and daydream • Controlling, bossy • Promiscuous	• Ashamed of situation and where they live • Developmentally delayed • School phobic (want to be with parents— fear of abandonment) • Poor organizational skills • Poor ability to conceptualize • Difficulty finishing what they start

which school the child would be attending. Or parents may be so caught up in concerns about family survival that facilitating the transfer of records is not high on their list of priorities. Even if the information is sent, the bureaucratic wheels turn slowly, so that the chances are slim that the new school will receive the records promptly.

What does the teacher do in such cases? The logical response is to talk with the student, learning as much as possible, and then schedule him/her for scholastic assessment. The problem then arises that these evaluations must also be scheduled or planned in advance and require the luxury of time. But time is the very thing that the teacher and the homeless student do *not* have. The student may be gone tomorrow— with no more information and more frustration for the student and the next school.

This problem calls upon teachers to use their own informal diagnostic skills and also to access the services quickly available in the school. It is wise to create a series of competencies for the grade level in which you teach. What do you hope the child will be able to do? One teacher created a brief assessment packet, including questions she could ask and tools to assess students' knowledge. She initiated the process for a more complete and formal assessment, but in the interim the student was able to begin an educational program.

This teacher kept her own records on the student's progress. When

Table 3
Frustrations for Homeless Students and
Their Teachers* in School

For Students	For Teachers
• Ashamed of where they live (especially if at a shelter)	• Students may have lived in many places, attending different schools with different methods
• Teased by other students about homelessness, hygiene, inabilities	• No school records
• Often feel misunderstood by parents	• Must assess educational needs without prior record input
• Difficulties in adjusting to new school magnified by situation	• Must do quick assessment of student as formal measures are too time-consuming
• No place to do homework (or quiet place to themselves)	• Knowledge that student will move soon
• Developmental delay augments feelings of failure	• Student may have difficulty trusting
	• Other students may react negatively
	• Inability to contact parents in an emergency
	• Parents often emotionally unavailable, too caught up in their own needs
	• Homework can be an issue

*And other school personnel.

she learned the child was about to leave, she made several copies of each report and paper. One copy she presented to the mother, instructing her clearly to give it to the next teacher. Another copy was placed in the student's record, and the third copy the teacher kept.

Another technique has proved particularly useful in transferring student records:

"I addressed a postcard to my school," the teacher told us, "and gave this prestamped card to the mother. The card said on the back:

Please transfer my child's records to:_____.

I asked the mother to sign it then and when the child was enrolled in another school to write the name of the school on the card and drop it in the mailbox. I realized that not all parents could follow through but this one did."

25

Shelter staff may also be of assistance in the transfer of school records. Many directors or case managers are willing to assist the parent in seeing that the transfer takes place.

An issue that often causes problems for homeless students is that of transportation to school. One eastern city has adopted a way to deal with this problem. Worcester, Massachusetts, provides transportation for homeless students to their last attended neighborhood school if the parents request this service. Transportation is guaranteed for the remainder of the school year. Such a plan provides more stability for the student, allowing him/her to continue with familiar settings and people. In some cities, shelters will agree to provide rides for students to get to school. It is important to explore all the options. The transition from school to school creates not only a logistical problem, but also an emotional one for the student. Schools have different rules, different expectations, and different personalities. Students who arrive with their peers at the beginning of the year have the support of others to discover these differences. The student who drifts in at midterm may feel totally at a loss. A brief chat about the new school or a carefully chosen peer as a guide may help. Moving about creates other issues as well. Students may feel anxious about the instability of their circumstances. They might not fully understand the implications of their lifestyles or have fears based on past experiences.

One principal described an experience with a third grader who came to her school:

> The little girl was brought in by her mother who left her in the classroom. The child panicked, screaming and crying—totally out of control. She had to be physically restrained. I took her to my office to calm her down. It took me half an hour to get her to the point where I could even get her to talk to me.
>
> I learned then that she had been abandoned by her mother many times in the past. What she experienced in that moment of separation was a feeling that she would be abandoned again. The child felt overwhelmed. I had her call the mother at the shelter to have the mother assure her that she had not left her, that at the end of the day she would be there to pick her up. Incidents like this make it immediately apparent that dealing with homeless children is not just an academic issue.

After numerous moves, homeless students, may have consciously or unconsciously decided they cannot trust others—"a friend made is a friend who will soon be left behind." Therefore they may find it difficult to make friends. They may see adults as people who will move on or disappoint them, and they may be reluctant to warm up to teachers or to cooperate with them. The only solution is patience and encouragement. The student who knows that the door is still open to a relationship, in spite of an initial inability to accept it, may eventually come around.

PROBLEMS WITH STUDIES

It is the role of teachers to make available to the homeless student whatever educational services they can access. Recognizing that students are homeless through no fault of their own may help teachers understand their need for an advocate. Many students from shelters are in inner-city schools—schools that, because of their location and population, *do* offer a myriad of services. For example, Chapter I services provide regular tutorial programs in reading and mathematics and can be made available to these students. Support personnel within the school (such as guidance and special education specialists) can be important resources. In addition, shelter personnel will often work with the school in the educational interest of the children.

One issue, which may stem from the transient quality of their lives, is the inability of some homeless students to finish their work. Since teachers tend to grade work on the whole rather than on the amount that has been completed correctly, the student who cannot finish a task, for whatever reason, suffers.

> Jess was consistently failing math. When the teacher studied his papers, however, he realized that what Jess *had* completed was correct. The issue was that he had not finished his assignments. It finally became obvious that this failing student was actually capable beyond the work he had been assigned, and was bored.

Of course, in some cases, students do not finish because the work is too difficult rather than too easy, or there may be other reasons.

As Coles (5) observed:

> Migrant boys and girls are quite willing to interrupt their particular tasks—for instance, the doing of a picture or the playing of various games with me—for any number of reasons. It is not that they are agitated or anxious or unable to concentrate and finish what they start ... one has to see the habits of these children as vastly responsive to the habits of their parents. If parents take in their stride (because they have learned they must) the necessity for constantly moving from one field to another, from one responsbility to another, each of which can only be partially fulfilled by any given person and indeed requires a whole field of people, then it is only natural that the children of migrants will experience no great need to stay with things, to work at them endlessly

and stubbornly or indeed consistently. Always the child has learned, there is the next place, the next journey, the next occasion. (pp. 94–95)

For still other students, unfinished tasks may be related to unorganized lifestyles or anxiety about their situation. In all cases, it is important to discern the reason for incomplete work.

Students who move from school to school may be missing the opportunity to acquire basic skills. Wanda, for example, left her school before her third grade class had begun to study multiplication tables. Her next school had completed this basic bit of learning early in the year. In one high school Toby entered, history was a sophomore-level course. The next school expected that students had learned the basics of history in junior high school. Graduation was denied until students could pass a basic competency test in history based on information Toby had never received.

An assessment based upon a set of expected competencies may tell the teacher in what areas the student will need remedial work. It is important, however, to remember and to convey to the student that these problems are often created by the system's inconsistencies rather than the student's failure.

But even when students have been given the basics, anxiety and confusion over their life situation may promote barriers to learning. In such cases, a referral to the guidance counselor or other counselor may free up the student's energy for schoolwork. Bassuk and Rubin (1) found a high incidence of depression that hampered students' ability to learn. These researchers also noted a high potential for serious developmental delay in homeless students. Of their samples, 43 percent of the students were failing or performing below-average work, 25 percent were in special classes, and 43 percent had repeated a grade (p. 283). Thus, most homeless students will require a referral for special educational services. Moreover, concentration can be hampered by hunger and poor nutrition. One concerned principal reports that she automatically signs up homeless students for free breakfast and lunch programs. Another teacher reports keeping snacks such as granola bars and raisins in her desk for the student who appears to need quick energy.

One issue mentioned again and again by teachers and others working with homeless students is homework. Given their lifestyle, there is too often little or no privacy, quiet, or space for these young people to do their homework. Teachers have worked out a variety of ways to compensate. A special study hall (distinguished in some manner from the stigma of detention) can be provided after school. One school librarian agreed to keep the library open after school for any student who needed a quiet setting for homework. City or town libraries may also be available for students to use as a quiet spot. Shelter directors, when notified by teachers of this problem, have made space and time available when students can be encouraged and often helped to do their homework. This issue may require some creativity, but the problem *can* be solved.

Teachers have also found a variety of ways to supply remedial help to their students. Out-of-date textbooks, and especially workbooks, can be given to students to practice basic skills. For some children, these discarded books may also provide a sense of ownership. Some teachers have made up worksheets or reminders of basic concepts that they have given to students to work on or keep.

Learning can be exciting for students, but when too many barriers arise, the same educational experience can augment feelings of failure. The goal with the homeless student, as with any other, is to remove as many barriers as possible.

PROBLEMS WITH PEERS

Danny stopped coming to school several days after he was enrolled. His teacher had observed him being teased by his peers and had tried to intervene. She guessed this was one reason behind his absence. A call home revealed that Danny and his mother lived at a local homeless shelter. He had valiantly attempted to conceal this fact from his peers, but when they discovered it, they taunted and ridiculed him. Finally, he could stand it no longer and refused to go to school.

To be sure, different is difficult for any child, but for one who is homeless, who is convinced that everyone else must surely have a home, the feeling is especially painful. Children not only feel different because they have no homes, but because they live in a shelter, a welfare hotel, or on the street. They often go to great lengths to conceal their homelessness. Hiding a secret such as this creates isolation, a fear of getting close to anyone lest they learn the secret. Often they begin to blame themselves.

At 14, Michael had repeated eighth grade twice. He was still not doing well in school. His father had lost his job; when he was unable to pay the rent, his family was evicted. Michael felt somehow responsible; he initiated fights in school, began smoking cigarettes to be more like his friends, and never had time to do his homework. When his family became homeless, he lost all sense of pride. He told no one that he lived in a shelter and began to isolate himself more and more. When he became involved in a fight at school, he was suspended for a short time. This only served to intensify his shame, guilt, and isolation.

When he was allowed to return to school he commented that if he had never been born his parents would not be in this situation. He verbalized his wish that he was dead.

Fortunately for Michael, his teacher recognized his depression and referred him for counseling. He was also placed in a classroom that encouraged self-expression, and his peers who had at one time been so important to him were helped to understand Michael's situation.

One way to help homeless children in their relationships with peers is to educate all students in the classroom about homelessness. Much care must be taken in the way in which this is done, however.

One school sent home a note with students asking for donated clothing for "the homeless shelter." Nine-year-old Sally said nothing when she came home to the shelter that day, but her letter was later found crumpled behind the couch. Fortunately communication between the shelter and the school transformed this unfortuante incident into a positive experience. In the end shelter children worked side by side with their peers sorting clothing that had been donated.

"Isn't this a neat shirt?" the shelter director overheard, as a friend helped Sally sort clothes. "It was mine, but now it's too small for me. You'd look great in it!" Giggles of admiration followed as Sally tried on the shirt.

Homeless students can be helped by enabling others to understand and share with them. As a migrant child in Coles's study (5) commented:

There was one teacher [who] said that as long as we were there in the class, she was going to ask everyone to join us; that's what she said, and we could teach other kids what we know and they could do the same with us. She showed the class where we traveled on the map and I told my daddy that I never before knew how far we went each year. . . . But when you look on the map and hear the other kids say they've never been that far, and they wish someday they could, then you think you've done something good, too, and they'll tell you in the recess that they've only seen where they live and we've been all over. (p. 52)

Some students whose lives have been different from others may have trouble differentiating when discussion of their experiences is appropriate. Their candor may actually create problems in their relationships with their peers.

30

Sondra, age six, was a victim of sexual abuse. Her mother had also been raped and was never able to deal with it. When Sondra was registered for first grade, she was eager to meet new friends. She had been in school only three hours when her mother received a call at the shelter at which they were staying. Sondra had announced in class that she had been sexually abused by a family member, much to the horror of her teacher and classmates.

For Sondra it was necessary that the shelter staff, school personnel, and her mother meet. Never able to handle her own experiences, Sondra's mother found this situation impossible to deal with. Despite the shelter staff's sensitive efforts to explain to Sondra that there were appropriate places to discuss her experiences, the damage had been done. Her mother's continued inability to talk with her intensified the problem. As her classmates found they were now uncomfortable with the child, Sondra began to have difficulties in school. She would often come home with headaches, cry with little provocation, and be unable to finish her work.

PROBLEMS WITH SELF-CONCEPT

Children who are having difficulty with their peers, who are isolated and perceive themselves to be different, who have feelings of failure and little sense of stability will probably not feel good about themselves. This negative self-concept is with homeless children from very early in life. Their parents feel badly about themselves and are often not able to communicate to their children that they are worthwhile. As each new assault on these small individuals happens, children feel less and less positive about themselves. Depression was a major finding in the Bassuk studies (1, 3); Bassuk and her colleagues felt that many of these children were in need of psychiatric evaluation.

Perhaps the best way to give homeless children an opportunity to feel good about themselves is to provide in the school setting the safety and stability not available to them outside of the classroom. Clair Angers, a school principal in Worcester, Massachusetts, and an advocate for homeless students, suggests:

One message I would give to teachers is, just imagine that these students are probably the most needy students you have ever encountered. Provide these children with a caring, stimulating environment that will be consistent. Make sure that they can expect the same behavior from you all the time. Communicate that you are going to provide a safe haven within the classroom—accepting them with all their deficiencies, all the difficulties they bring to the classroom. Start at that level and give them all you can give them whether it's for one week or one month. I think that the teacher can feel secure that for that one week or one month in that child's life he/she was safe—nurtured and provided with a consistent environment. That's a lot.

In addition to providing stability, it is important to help students engineer their own successes. Assigning them small tasks that they can complete and feel good about can help them feel better about themselves. Look for strengths in these intinerant students and help them develop them.

April's teacher discovered from her doodling that April had a real flare for drawing. The teacher provided the girl with paper, colored pencils, and an old art workbook that explained how to draw still life. The teacher's encouragement gave April a purpose. The girl's drawings would sustain her for the painful years to come.

Not all students have as tangible a talent to build upon as April, but each one can do something well. These strengths may be merely their readiness to please and help in class. Students should also be encouraged to recognize and appreciate their own strengths. Numerous books on enhancing self-concept in students are available (21, 23). These can be of assistance to teachers who work with homeless students.

These students can also be encouraged to recognize and express their feelings. This helps others to understand them. Exercises in class that encourage the expression of feelings may also open communication between homeless students and their peers. Table 4, Quick Reference for Classroom Tips, provides additional suggestions for helping these students.

Having homeless students in the classroom can admittedly be challenging, necessitating ingenuity, creativity, and patience. As mentioned earlier, students may communicate their frustrations through withdrawing or acting aggressively, for example. Yet it is important to remember that the school can be a vitally important part of the homeless child's life. School experiences can actually enable children to cope with their homelessness. As one teacher expressed it:

If I can give these children a stable, secure environment and a lot of TLC and understanding for just six hours a day, for however long they're in with me, maybe—just maybe—they'll come through their chaos with a little more ease. After all, we all need that safe island in a storm. We all need to know there is someone who really cares.

Table 4
Quick Reference for Classroom Tips

- Provide a stable environment.
- Provide structure.
- Allow personal possessions or space and encourage rights to them.
- Expect and unobtrusively monitor regressions.
- Assign projects that can be broken into small components to ensure at least some successes.
- Allow students to express fears.
- Allow students to express frustrations and allow opportunities to do so in other ways in addition to verbalizing (e.g., drawing).
- Make professional help quickly available (e.g., an informed school counselor).
- Be open to students' needs to talk about experiences without prying.
- Give students opportunities to see some of their experiences as positive (e.g., places they have traveled).
- Don't assume students know how to play. They may have to be taught how to do so.
- Be well informed about homelessness issues.

Chapter 4

WHAT THE TEACHER CAN DO OUTSIDE THE CLASSROOM

The most important thing teachers can do for their homeless students is to become educated on the subject of homelessness. Increasingly, schools are providing in-service training courses and speakers for staff. Some local colleges may also provide courses in homelessness (which might be used for continuing education credits). Within recent years, several helpful books and articles have appeared on the growing numbers of homeless families. Such works as *Rachel and her Children*, by Jonathan Kozol (12); *Uprooted Children*, by Robert Coles (5); *The Faces of Homelessness*, by Marjorie Hope and James Young (10); and *The Homeless in Contemporary Society*, by Richard Bingham, Roy Green and Sammis White (4) provide especially informative reading. Organizations dedicated to advocacy for the homeless and migrant workers (see Appendix B) may suggest other pertinent materials.

Teachers might also visit and develop relationships with local shelters. Shelter staff may agree to provide training in issues of homelessness, or give those interested a tour and explanation of shelter services. Those who really want to learn about the working of a shelter and the problems of the homeless might consider volunteering their time to the shelter in some capacity.

It is often beneficial to students for schools and shelters to collaborate beyond a simple information/training basis. One school that enrolls a large number of homeless students has developed a reciprocal relationship with the shelter in which these young people are usually housed. The shelter director sits on the school advisory board, while the school principal is a member of the shelter's board. This arrangement facilitates collaboration about policies as well as individuals.

Teachers may also be in a position to meet with the parents of homeless students. It is often frustrating when these parents are not as responsive as teachers believe they should be. For example, they may be difficult to reach when the child is ill; they may fail to come in for conferences. It is important to realize, however, that while the children come to school, the parents are deeply engaged in pursuing issues of survival (e.g., where the family members will sleep, what they will eat, how they will live). The parents' energies are often exhausted before they are finally able to meet with school personnel. Remembering that these parents are as much victims—whether of society's injustices, or of their own inadequacies—as their children may help in dealing with them. In the face of what is often interpreted as indifference, it would be easy to make decisions about the children's education for the parents. But these parents need to feel in control. Their lives are characterized by feeling out of control. Persistence may be necessary in getting them involved. And as one principal commented:

> Along with persistence is the need to be nonjudgmental. We have no right to pass judgment on their lives. We must also realize that they may in fact not have enough energy left over to make decisions and handle problems. Seeming to criticize already overwhelmed parents will do nothing but augment their feelings of failure to the detriment of the children.

When dealing with parents, teachers should not be afraid to involve others who may support the parents. For example, parents often come to depend upon shelter staff, who might welcome teachers' input. It may be helpful to meet with a shelter worker or director along with the parent, but it is vital to give the parent that choice.

Both homeless parents and their children need political advocates as well. In 1987 Congress passed the Stewart B. McKinney Homeless Assistance Act (P.L. 100-77), which promised over a billion dollars in emergency relief for the poor. An amendment authorized the Department of Education to provide for the educational needs of homeless children. Initially funds were set aside for planning to ensure that these children's educational needs were met. State offices were urged to assess the needs of their particular areas. But the implementation of actual programs will take time—and public support. Organizations such as the Children's Defense Fund, the National Coalition for the Homeless, the National Conference for the Homeless, and the National Conference of Mayors (see Appendix B for addresses) can advise those who are interested how their help could be most beneficial to homeless children and their families.

Fighting the problems of homelessness will be a major battle for the future. Estimates are that the situation will get worse before it gets better. Teachers—by virtue of their understanding of and close contact with students—are in an excellent position to make a significant difference in the lives of the homeless students in their classrooms.

GLOSSARY OF TERMS

Homeless Shelters—Centers that offer temporary housing for homeless individuals, families, or people who are active substance abusers. These shelters are often funded by local churches, departments of public welfare, or private organizations. They usually offer meals and board to their guests. Guests are expected to search for permanent housing while staying in the shelter.

Types of Shelters:

Individual Shelters—House individuals, male or female, who are employed or are searching for work. Individuals may be involved in an alcohol or drug program. They are also actively searching for a change in their life.

Family Shelters—House only families—women and child(ren), intact families, or pregnant women. Family shelters deal with housing issues, parenting, housekeeping, nutritional and budgeting issues. They also advocate for the homeless children in their area through the school system.

Wet Shelters—Offer shelter to active users of alcohol or drugs who have not fit into the sheltering system of searching for permanent housing. Wet shelters also offer some type of training skills and a drug and alcohol program to teach nondependence.

Welfare Hotels—Used as a last resort in housing homeless people because of the lack of program and the nonstructure the hotels provide. Some are designed specifically for the use of the homeless; some—like the Martinique Hotel in New York City (see Kozol [12]) or the Pitts Hotel in Washington, D.C.—have been criticized for deplorable conditions. The cost of using these hotels is far greater than shelters. Housing a family in a hotel for a period of time is much more costly than providing family members with temporary shelters or some type of permanent housing.

AFDC (Aid to Families with Dependent Children)—Aid supplied through the department of public welfare, providing the applicant meets all the requirements requested by the case manager. The applicant must go through a series of required programs offered through the department—for example, Employment Training, Child Support Unit, Healthy Choices. All states offer different programs to AFDC recipients. Eligibility requires that a child be present in the household. Usually the children in the family are members of a one-parent household.

FEMA (Federal Emergency Money Assistance)—Available to certified agencies to distribute monies to qualifying people for back rent payable to the landlord. FEMA monies can also be used to avoid evictions that lead to homelessness. Income level and rent receipts qualify an individual. FEMA monies are also used to feed people   at soup kitchens or food pantries that distribute dry goods and meat to the needy.

G.R. (General relief)—Offered through the department of public welfare to single individuals who are unable to work. Paperwork must be presented to the case manager proving the applicant's inability to work.

HUD (Housing and Urban Development)—A federal agency that builds low-income housing. The buildings are available through local housing authorities and house only low-income people.

SRO (Single Room Occupancy)—One room rented to a single individual. Usually no cooking facilities are available in the room and bathroom facilities are shared by all tenants on the floor. Single rooms usually rent for $50 to $90 weekly and require some type of security deposit. The majority of these single rooms are not kept up to safety and health standards. Thus, single room occupancy is harder and harder to find for homeless individuals.

APPENDIXES

A. AN AMERICAN TRAGEDY: HOMELESS CHILDREN
by Mary Hatwood Futrell

Washington, D.C.—A national coalition was recently formed to address the issue of the homeless in America. At a news conference on Wednesday, April 19, 1989, the group outlined a series of activities to take place over the next several months.

Mary Hatwood Futrell, President of the National Education Asociation, addressed the educational needs of homeless children.

MHF: I am here today to bring attention to an American tragedy—our homeless children.

The fastest growing segment of the homeless are families with children. The National Coalition for the Homeless estimates that between 500,000 and 750,000 children are homeless. I suspect the true number is closer to 1 million.

Homeless children endure, of course, the stress of being without a permanent home. But they also suffer from poor nutrition, inadequate medical care, and low self-esteem.

These children, reports the National Coalition for the Homeless, are three times as likely as other children to develop respiratory ailments, ear infections, heart problems, anemia, neurological disorders, and illnesses that could be avoided if they had received the standard childhood inoculations.

Even more shocking: Many of these children are being denied a free, public education—a gift so many of us take for granted.

In fact, over 40 percent of school-age homeless children do not attend school. Until recently, many school districts required a permanent address for registration purposes. And a permanent address is the one thing homeless children do not have!

Other barriers also keep these children from schools. Homeless children lack transportation. Their health and school records are inadequate.

The situation is nothing less than a national tragedy.

We must all work together—diligently—to assure that no American youngster spends another night without shelter, that no American student is denied access to our public schools.

For now, these are children condemned to homelessness. But they need not be condemned to ignorance. They need not be denied an education, need not be sentenced to a life of intense despair.

The 1.9 million members of the National Education Association are committed to ensuring that all of America's children have access to our public schools.

NEA and its affiliates have been reaching out to the homeless youngsters in our communities. Teachers in Portsmouth, Virginia have adopted a shelter for homeless women and children and provide tutoring for the children.

And school staffs are working in special schools devoted to homeless students in Tacoma, Washington, Santa Clara, California, and Salt Lake City, Utah.

We live in the greatest country in the world, the United States of America. Yet too many of our children are disenfranchised from the American dream. Our nation cannot build its future on a foundation of child neglect.

B. ADVOCACY ORGANIZATIONS FOR THE HOMELESS

Association of Junior Leagues, Inc. (660 First Avenue, New York, NY 10016 [212-683-1515]), is an international organization of women committed to promoting voluntarism and improving the community through the effective action and leadership of trained volunteers. Its purpose is exclusively educational and charitable. It reaches out to all young women, regardless of race, religion, or national origin, who demonstrate an interest and commitment to voluntarism. AJL recently cosponsored an issues forum on the homeless with the Johnson Foundation. A summary of that forum is contained in the monograph *The New Homeless: Women, Children and Families.*

Center for Law and Education, Inc. (14 Appian Way, Cambridge, MA 02138 [617-495-4666]), is funded by the Legal Services Corporation, Washington, D.C., to serve as a national legal support center on the education problems of low-income students. This organization focuses directly on education of homeless children. Its newsletters are distributed free to each legal services program's main and branch offices, to specialists in education advocacy, and to subscribers to other center periodicals.

Child Welfare League of America (440 First Street, NW, Washington DC 20001 [202-638-2952], founded in 1920, is a federation of 500 public and private child care organizations working with children and their families on critical issues such as child abuse, teen pregnancy, day care, homeless children, and advocacy. In 1987, CWLA conducted a national study of barriers to homeless children in registering and attending school. The more than 125,000 professionals who work at CWLA member agencies help 2 million children and their families annually.

Children's Defense Fund (122 C Street, NW, Washington, DC 20001 [202-628-8787]) is a private organization supported by foundations, corporate grants, and individual donations. While its main offices are in Washington, DC, CDF is a national organization that reaches out to towns and cities across the country to monitor the effects of changes in national and state policies and to help people and organizations who are concerned with children. CDF maintains state offices in Minnesota, Mississippi, Ohio, Texas, and Virginia.

CDF focuses on programs and policies that affect large numbers of children, rather than helping families on a case-by-case basis. It gathers data and disseminates information on key issues affecting children, including information on state and federal policies affecting homeless children and their families. CDF is in the process of developing an agenda for homeless children.

Council of Chief State School Officers (400 North Capitol Street, NW, Washington, DC 20001 [202-393-8161]) is a nationwide nonprofit organization of the 56 officials who head departments of public education in the 50 states, the District of Columbia, and the five extra-state jurisdictions. CCSSO seeks its members' consensus on major education issues and expresses their views to civic and professional organizations, to federal agencies, to Congress, and to the public. Through its standing and special committees, the Council responds to a broad range of educational concerns and provides leadership on major education issues. The CCSSO Policy on Assuring School Success for Students at Risk states:

> In addition to advances within the education system, there must be new harmony of education and related support programs. Ill health, poor housing, inadequate nutrition, unsafe streets—these promote the condition of risk. These conditions are to be changed together with school improvement. Evoking change is a multiagency responsibility. It requires reaching out from education to other systems and actions by public authorities who are responsible for these combinations of service. A commitment to such outreach must be made.

National Coalition for the Homeless (105 East 22d Street, New York, NY 10010 [212-460-8110]) is a federation of individuals, agencies, and organizations committed to the principles that decent shelter and housing and adequate food are fundamental rights in a civilized society. It serves as clearinghouse to share information and resources. Some key publications are *Broken Lives: Denial of Education to Homeless Children*, and A briefing paper for Presidential Candidates: *Homelessness in the United States: Background and Federal Response.*

National School Boards Association (1680 Duke Street, Alexandria, VA 22314 [703-838-6722]) is a federation of 49 state associations of local school boards, plus the Hawaii State School Board and the boards of education of the District of Columbia and the Virgin Islands. It represents 97,000 school board members across the country who set policy for 15,300 public school districts. Its policies on children at risk who need special programs and services include homeless children who are denied education.

U.S. Conference of Mayors (1620 I Street, NW, Washington, DC 20006 [202-293-7330]), an organization of mayors of cities of over 30,000 population, surveyed 26 major cities in 1987 to assess the status of hunger, homelessness, and poverty in urban America. The survey sought information from each city on (1) the demand for emergency food assistance and shelter, and the capacity of local agencies to meet that demand; (2) the causes of hunger and homelessness and the demographics of the populations experiencing these problems; (3) the status of affordable housing for low-income people; (4) economic conditions relating to poverty and unemployment; (5) the impact of national economic recovery on these problems; and (6) the outlook for these problems in 1988.

C. SAMPLE FORMS

Student Assessment Form
XYZ School

Basic Student Information

Name: _____

Age: _____   Grade: _____

Teacher: _____

Counselor: _____

School in which student is presently enrolled:

_____

School enrollment date when student entered shelter: _____

School telephone number: _____

Student Background Information

List names and addresses of schools student has attended in last two years (with dates):

1. _____

_____

2. _____

_____

3. _____

_____

Were student's records available for transfer to this school?

     Yes_____   No_____

If no,

    1.   Where can records be obtained?

_____

2. When will records be available? _____

3. If no records can be obtained, will student be accepted in this school?

_____

Immunization Records

Medical History

1. Is student developing properly? _____

2. Is the grade level too difficult for the student to complete work?

_____

3. Is the student seeing a doctor?_____
   Is the student caught up on shots? _____

Prevention Measures for Student's Education

Does the student have any special learning disabilities? If so, please specify.

_____

_____

_____

Does the student need special teachers or counselors?

_____

_____

What do you see as a potential problem for the student's needs?

_____

_____

Is the student signed up for free breakfast and lunch programs?

_____

Is milk or juice provided for the kindergarten-age child?

_____

43

Transportation

What type of transportation does the student have to attend school?

_____

1. Where is the student picked up?_____

2. What time is the pickup?_____

Does the education system need to arrange transportation?

Yes_____   No_____

If yes, what date did school staff call and when does transportation start?

_____

Followup

Has release been signed to secure above information from school authorities?

_____

Date signed by parent: _____

Notify school that family has moved from shelter and where the student is now attending school.

Check with new school to make sure student is registered and attending.

File opened on this student: _____
                                                    (date)

File closed on this student: _____
                                                    (date)

Overall Observation of the Student

School attendance: _____

Cooperation: _____

Staff member's signature:

_____
                                                    (date)

Parent Release Form
for School Records

I, _____ , parent

of _____ , wish to
have my child's records transferred to

_____ . My new address is

_____ and my child will

attending _____ School.

Thank you for providing educational services to my child.

Signed: _____

Date: _____

Parent Release Form
for Shelter-School Information

I, _____ , hereby give the Salvation
Army Booth Home Staff permission to secure information from
_____ School for
my child, _____ . The purpose of this
release is to give information between the shelter and the school in helping my
child to cope with this unstable time of homelessness. Information requested
will include but will not be limited to—

1. Medical records
2. Problems of cooperation in the classroom
3. Release of records when permanent housing is secured
4. Transportation
5. School Issues

Date Signed: _____

Parent's Name: _____
                      (Please print)

Signature: _____

Child's Name: _____
                      (Please print)

Signature: _____

BIBLIOGRAPHY

1. Bassuk, E., and Rubin, L. "Homeless Children: A Neglected Population." *American Journal of Orthopsychiatry* 57, no. 2 (April 1987): 279–86.
2. Bassuk, E.; Rubin, L.; and Lauriat, A. S. "Characteristics of Sheltered Homeless Families." *American Journal of Public Health* 76 (September 1986): 1097–1101.
3. Bassuk, E. E.; Lauriat, A.; and Rubin, L. "Homeless Families." In *Homelessness: Critical Issues for Policy and Practice.* pp. 20–33. Boston: Boston Foundation, 1987
4. Bingham, R. D.; Green, R. E.; and White, S. B. *The Homeless in Contemporary Society.* Newbury Park, Calif.: Sage Publishing, 1987.
5. Coles, R. *Uprooted Children: The Early Life of Migrant Farm Workers.* Pittsburgh: University of Pittsburgh Press, 1970.
6. Committee on Judiciary, U.S. Senate, Ninety-sixth Congress. *Homeless Youth: The Saga of "Pushouts" and "Throwaways" in America.* Washington, D.C.: U.S. Government Printing Office, 1980.
7. Fried, M. "Endemic Stress: The Psychology of Resignation and Politics of Scarcity." *American Journal of Orthopsychiatry* 52 (January 1982): 6–8.
8. Gewirtzman, R., and Fodor, I. "The Homeless Child at School: From Welfare Hotel to Classroom." *Child Welfare* 66, no. 3 (May–June 1987): 237–45.
9. Haus, A., ed. *Working with Homeless People: A Guide for Staff and Volunteers.* New York: Columbia University Community Services, 1988.
10. Hope, M., and Young, J. *The Faces of Homelessness.* Lexington, Mass.: Lexington Books, 1986.
11. Interstate Migrant Education Council (IMEC). "Migrant Education: A Consolidated View." Denver, Colo.: Interstate Migrant Education Council, Education Commission of the States, 1987. Available from Suite 300, 1860 Lincoln St., Denver, CO 80295. (303) 830–3680.
12. Kozol, J. *Rachel and Her Children.* New York: Crown Publishing, 1988.
13. Maza, P. L., and Hall, J. A. *Homeless Children and their Families: A Preliminary Study.* Washington D.C.: Child Welfare League of America, 1988.
14. McChesney, K. "Families: The New Homeless." *Family Professional* 1, no. 1 (Winter 1986): 6–7.
15. Phillips, M.; De Chillo, N.; Kronenfeld, D.; and Middleton-Jeter, V. "Homeless Families: Services Make a Difference." *Social Casework* (January 1988): 48–53.
16. Plato, Kathleen. "Program for Migrant Children's Education: A National Profile." Olympia, Wash.: National Association of State Directors of Migrant Education, Washington Office of State Superintendent of Public Instruction, 1984.

17. Price, V. "Runaways and Homeless Street Youth." In *Homelessness: Critical Issues for Policy and Practice*, pp. 24–28. Boston, Mass.: Boston Foundation, 1987.
18. Rodriquez, A. F., and Gilbert, M. B. "MENTE Spells Success for Migrant Students." *Science Teacher* 52, no. 7 (October 1985): 29–31.
19. Roth, D.; Bean, J.; Lust, N.; Saveanu, T. *Homeless in Ohio: A Study of People in Need*. Columbus: Department of Mental Health, Office of Program Evaluation and Research, 1985.
20. Sanchez, R. "For Homeless, School No Shelter from Shame." *Washington Post*, December 1988.
21. Silvernail, David L. *Developing Positive Student Self-Concept*. 2d ed. Washington, D.C.: National Education Association, 1985.
22. Toelle, M. E. "Children in Transition." *Children Today* 17, no. 5 (September–October 1988): 27–31.
23. Wells, Harold C., and Canfield, Jack. *One Hundred Ways to Enhance Self-Concepts in the Classroom: Handbook for Teachers and Parents*. Englewood Cliffs, N.J.: Prentice-Hall, 1983.
24. Young, P. "The Human Cost of Unemployment." *Sociology and Social Research* 17 (March–April 1933): 363. Cited in Bingham, Green, and White, *The Homeless in Contemporary Society*. Newbury Park, Calif.: Sage Publishing, 1987.

NEA Policy
on Education for
Homeless Children

Resolution C-33. Education for Homeless Children and Youth

The National Education Association believes that education must be provided for all children and youth, including those without a permanent legal address.

The Association advocates the right of all students to an education, adequate housing, and health care.

The Association reecognizes the need for cooperation between school and community groups in meeting the needs of homeless children and youth.

The Association urges its affiliates to seek legislation to ensure equal educational opportunities for all children and youth. (88, 89)